Chocolate Cakes

20 FABULOUSLY INDULGENT CAKES

TOM PHILLIPS

NH
NEW HOLLAND

First published in 2005 by New Holland Publishers (UK) Ltd
London · Cape Town · Sydney · Auckland

Garfield House, 86–88 Edgware Road, London, W2 2EA, United Kingdom
www.newhollandpublishers.com

80 McKenzie Street, Cape Town 8001, South Africa

14 Aquatic Drive, Frenchs Forest, NSW 2086, Australia

218 Lake Road, Northcote, Auckland, New Zealand

ISBN 1 84330 978 5

Senior Editor: Clare Hubbard
Editorial Direction: Rosemary Wilkinson
Design: AG&G Books
Photographer: Shona Wood
Production: Ben Byram-Wigfield

1 3 5 7 9 10 8 6 4 2

Reproduction by Colourscan Overseas Co. Pte Ltd, Singapore
Printed and bound in Malaysia by Times Offset (M) Sdn Bhd

Note
The author and publishers have made every effort to ensure that all instructions
given in this book are safe and accurate, but they cannot accept liability for any
resulting injury or loss or damage to either property or person, whether direct or
consequential and howsoever arising.

Acknowledgements
I would like to thank the following individuals for their invaluable help and without
whom the completion of this book would not have been possible:
My wife Lorraine, for her encouragement, patience and proofreading.
Staff at Hannah's of Quorn for repeatedly testing and providing feedback on all of the recipes.
Clare Hubbard, editor, for her continued support, guidance and constructive feedback.
Sarah's Flowers of Quorn for providing the fresh flowers.
Jo Willis at Barry Callebaut (UK) Ltd for supplying supporting literature and the quality chocolate.

Picture credits
Pg 5, Barry Callebaut (UK) Ltd

Contents

Introduction

> Chocolate brings to mind marvellous gratification:
> Children . . . . *relish it*
> Lovers . . . . *share it*
> Chocoholics . . . . *stash it*
> Stockbrokers . . . . *dabble in it*
> Wealthy people . . . . . . *lavish in it*
> Pregnant women . . . . . *crave it*
> Designers . . . . *market it*
> Women . . . . *need it*
> Sensualists . . . . *indulge in it*
> Pagans . . . . *worship it*
> Hedonists . . . . *enjoy it*
> Everyone . . . . *eats it*
>
> ELAINE SHERMAN, WRITER

Enthusiasm and interest in working with (and eating!) chocolate has never been greater. Skills and techniques have developed over the years in an effort to satisfy the increasingly hungry customer – not only hungry for chocolate, but also for more novel and innovative chocolate creations. In addition, a whole range of new products and ingredients are now widely available. Such developments allow the beginner the success that only the most experienced and professional chocolatier could have enjoyed in the past. There has never been a better time to experiment with chocolate, there appears to be no limits to the possibilities.

This book presents 20 exciting and innovative chocolate cakes for all occasions, including birthdays, weddings, Christmas, Easter, Valentine's Day and more. Each cake has simple step-by-step instructions and photographs. Firstly though, the book provides a general introduction to chocolate – it is important that you read this section as you will need this basic knowledge before you make any of the cakes. Have fun making (and indulging in) these creations – they are guaranteed to satisfy the needs of even the most serious chocoholic. I hope that the book will give you the confidence to create your own designs. Challenge yourself to experiment and explore with new ideas and creations; you will soon discover that the possibilities really are endless!

All About Chocolate

THE HISTORY

"As an act of love, Quetzalcoatl bestowed on his people (the Toltecs) a little shrub that had, until then, belonged exclusively to the gods. The ...cocoa tree... was planted in the rugged fields... the goddess of love and happiness adorned it with beautiful blossoms."

ELAINE GONZALEZ, ARTIST

More than two hundred years ago, the great Swedish botanist Carolus Linnaeus christened the cocoa tree *Theobroma cocoa*, 'food of the gods cocoa'. Truly, chocolate is the closest thing we have to ambrosia. Chocolate started its culinary life as a frothy drink called *chocolatl*, drunk by the Olmec, Maya and Aztec peoples as far back as 2000 B.C. They believed that the cocoa tree belonged to the gods and the fruits were an offering from the gods to man. This precious commodity was not to remain the property of the New World for very long and, after being discovered by Columbus in 1502, was taken back with him to Spain. The Spaniards used the Aztec recipe but added chillies and other hot spices. Sugar and vanilla were also added, making it more palatable. The Spanish remained the sole European consumers until 1615 when a wedding between a Spanish princess and King Louis XIII of France brought the chocolate fashion to France. Towards the end of the seventeenth century, chocolate became a common commodity throughout Europe. By the mid-eighteenth century, it was also popular in America. Coffee houses that served cocoa gained in popularity and became meeting places, serving a similar function to the bars and cafes of today.

The late eighteenth to early nineteenth centuries saw many new developments. In 1795 an English man, Dr Joseph Fry, used a steam engine to grind the cocoa beans and started to manufacture chocolate on a larger scale. In 1828, a Dutch man, C.J. Van Houten, invented the cocoa press to squeeze the fat from the beans, thereby making the drink more digestible, and nearly 50 years later, a Swiss man, Daniel Peter, successfully added milk to produce solid chocolate. A few years on, and again in Switzerland, Rodolfe Lindt introduced the process of conching, which involved heating and agitating the chocolate over a period of time. This resulted in more refined chocolate, which, with the addition of extra cocoa butter, allowed it to be poured into moulds, thus paving the way for chocolate confectionery as we know it today.

FROM BEAN TO BAR

Cocoa trees grow in a narrow belt along the equator. They are fragile and need constant warmth, rainfall and shelter from the wind and sun. As a result, they are grown alongside 'shade trees' such as coconut, banana and plantain. The ripe pods, which come in many shapes, colours and sizes are harvested with great care, cut in half and the creamy white beans inside scooped out and piled in baskets with a covering of banana leaves. They are then left to ferment for five to seven days. The sweet, fleshy pulp, or baba, surrounding the beans provides the sugar for this natural fermentation process. The residue of the fruit evaporates and leaves behind traces of acetic acid allowing the beans to develop their characteristic colour and flavour. The beans are then sun dried on bamboo mats for about six days before being graded and sorted, packed into sacks and distributed to chocolate factories worldwide.

The cocoa tree.

At the factory the beans are checked for quality, then roasted at a temperature of 120–140°C (250–280°F), to bring out their intense flavour. The next process is winnowing, where the outer layer of the bean is cracked and blown away, leaving the inner seed, which is transformed into chocolate. What happens next depends on the type of chocolate required. Cheap chocolate is made quickly. The cocoa butter is removed and replaced with hydrogenated vegetable fats as well as artificial additives. These fats have a higher melting point and leave a greasy residue that sticks to the palate after you have eaten the chocolate.

Better chocolate is milled through a series of metal rollers and conches, which pummel it between granite rollers at a temperature of 50–80°C (120–175°F) for up to a week. Various flavours are added at this stage including pure vanilla, cloves and cinnamon. The longer the chocolate is refined in this way, the smaller the particle size and the smoother the chocolate. Also, more acetic acid will evaporate, removing the bitterness, resulting in a mellower flavour.

The finest chocolate has extra cocoa butter added to make it smoother and quicker to melt in the mouth. Sugar is also added. (The amount of sugar added is declared on the dark chocolate wrapping. For example, 70 percent cocoa solids has 30 percent sugar, so tastes bitter. Sixty percent cocoa solids has 40 percent sugar so tastes sweeter.) Milk chocolate has milk added with the sugar. White chocolate is cocoa butter, with flavourings, milk and sugar added.

WHY DO WE LOVE CHOCOLATE?

"Good chocolate won't make you sick. It won't even make you fat. Look at me, and I eat it all day long."
ROBERT LINXE, CHOCOLATIER

As well as chocolate looking and tasting so good, there are many other reasons for indulging. Good quality chocolate:

1 is a nutritious and easily digested food containing many minerals, vitamins and complex alkaloids which enhance health and well being;

2 can boost energy levels and increase mental alertness;

3 contains cocoa butter which has been proven to lower cholesterol levels;

4 contains theobromine and valeric acid which stimulate the nervous system and lower blood pressure;

5 contains phenylethylamine, this is a natural anti-depressant which will therefore influence your mood;

6 is low in sugar and has a low glycaemic index, meaning it keeps you feeling full for longer and maintains steady blood glucose levels;

7 is rich in antioxidants, which help to destroy free radicals and boost the immune system, both important factors in the prevention of cancer;

8 is rich in flavinoids and other chemical compounds known to reduce the likelihood of deep vein thrombosis and strokes.

APPRECIATING AND CHOOSING CHOCOLATE

"When you work with chocolate every day, mediocrity is abhorred."
BILL YOSSES, PASTRY CHEF

Your choice of chocolate depends on what you want to use it for. Do you intend to make fine desserts or truffles? Ganaches or sauces? Decorative moulding or artistic chocolate shapes? It is also a matter of personal preference, but I believe preference should be informed by knowledge. In this respect, learn how to read labels. Whilst not all product labels are informative, more and more companies are beginning to provide important information relevant to consumers. In particular, try to establish the following:

The origin of the cocoa beans
The very best chocolate will name the type and origin of the beans. This is important for those who appreciate the subtle differences in taste between different beans and origins.

Total cocoa content Cocoa is what makes chocolate taste like chocolate. Standard supermarket bars typically have a low cocoa content and are supplemented with fillers and sugars. Good quality chocolate has at least the basic 35 percent cocoa content. Premium chocolate usually has much more, ranging from 41 percent for first class milk chocolate, to 70–75 percent for intense, dark (bittersweet) chocolate. However, bear in mind that a a high cocoa content does not necessarily equate to quality.

Fat The type and amount of fat is also crucial. In European law, only chocolate that contains cocoa butter can be labelled 'chocolate'. If it contains any vegetable fats, it must be given an alternative name such as 'chocolate cake covering' or 'chocolate flavoured compound'. The best chocolate has extra cocoa butter added and is called couverture. Standards vary, but in Europe only chocolate with over 31 percent cocoa butter can be classed as couverture. The extra cocoa butter gives a superior shine and snap. Personally, I only ever use couverture in my work because it gives quality taste, shine and hardness that cannot be achieved with other types of chocolate. I strongly encourage you to spend a little time mastering the techniques of working with couverture. It really will be time well spent, as it will enhance the appearance and flavour of your cakes. It should be noted that delicate items such as bows and pipeouts can only successfully be made with couverture.

TYPES OF CHOCOLATE

Couverture This is the professional's choice. A fine quality pure chocolate with a high percentage of cocoa butter, giving it a high gloss finish and smooth taste. It must be tempered (see pages 8–9) before use in most cases. It is available in block or callet (drop) form and can be ordered in various viscosities depending on its use (i.e. hand dipping, moulding, with machinery etc.). It can be obtained from speciality chocolate shops and suppliers. Dark couverture ranges from sweet (semisweet), with 50 percent cocoa solids, to the more bitter (bitter-

Block chocolate and callets (drops).

sweet) chocolate with 75 percent cocoa solids. Milk couverture has powdered or condensed milk added. It ranges from very light and milky to a dark milk chocolate. White couverture is a mixture of cocoa butter, milk and sugar.

Eating chocolate There are many bars of chocolate gracing the super-market shelves which range in quality. They are primarily designed to be eaten as a bar, rather than to be melted down and made into other items. Most do not melt very smoothly. However, they can be used for making sauces and for flavouring buttercreams etc.

Baker's chocolate This is a blend of sugar, vegetable oils, cocoa and flavourings. It is often labelled as 'chocolate flavoured cake covering' or 'chocolate flavoured compound'. It has an inferior taste and shine and a soft consistency. As it contains no cocoa butter, it does not require

tempering before use. It is mainly used for coating cakes and biscuits. It can also be used for cutouts, runouts and for flooding cake drums.

Cocoa powder This is made from finely ground pure cocoa mass after the cocoa butter has been extracted. As it will mix readily with flour, it is the most effective way of giving baked goods a chocolate flavour.

Chocolate powder This has fewer cocoa solids than cocoa powder and has a milder, sweeter taste.

Chocolate know-how

For each cake, guidance is given as to which type(s) of chocolate can be used. At the same time, do not be afraid to experiment with the wide range that is available.

Basic Techniques

STORING CHOCOLATE

Chocolate can be stored successfully for up to a year, but because it is sensitive to humidity, odours and oxidation, it should be protected against light and air. Store it in a dark, dry, cool place at a constant temperature between 12–20°C (54–68°F), away from strong odours. Chocolate that is not stored correctly will not melt properly, will be difficult to work with and will be tainted with 'off' flavours.

MELTING CHOCOLATE

When melting, chocolate should never be placed in direct contact with the heat source. Chocolate should be melted at a temperature of between 40–45°C (100–110°F). Callets or blocks chopped into small pieces can be melted in:

1   the microwave. Use a low setting and stir the chocolate every so often to distribute the heat and prevent hotspots.

2   a double boiler. Use hot (but never boiling) water in the lower saucepan and slowly melt the chocolate. Neither steam nor water should come into contact with the chocolate, otherwise it will thicken and be rendered unusable.

3   a very low oven (50–100°C/ 120–210°F). Place the chocolate in a heatproof bowl and leave it in the oven until melted.

TEMPERING

Cocoa butter is one of the most chemically intricate and challenging fats. It contains three different fat molecules which become solid or liquid at three slightly different temperatures. This is why the sensation of chocolate melting in your mouth is so unlike anything else. It is also the reason why people often have difficulty working with quality chocolate.

Due to the different melting temperatures chocolate containing a significant amount of cocoa butter needs to be 'tempered' or 'pre-crystallized' before use. Through the tempering process the stable fat crystals that are hard and shiny are selected, omitting the softer, unstable crystals. This process happens by a sequence of heating, cooling and stirring until the ideal working temperature is achieved. Failure to temper correctly will result in the chocolate setting in a soft and unstable form, causing a bloom to appear on the surface.

There are three main methods of tempering chocolate, all of which can be used for dark (semisweet), milk and white chocolate. The only difference is that the final working temperature for white and milk chocolate – 30°C/85°F – is two degrees lower than for dark (semisweet) – 32°C/90°F. This is because they contain milk fats which affect the crystallization. Use a chocolate thermometer when tempering (see page 15). It is important that the working temperature is maintained. If the chocolate is allowed to cool too much or is overheated, you must melt and temper again.

The marble method This method requires a cool marble surface and is good for tempering blocks of chocolate.

1   Melt the chocolate at a temperature between 40–45°C (100–110°F).

2   Pour two-thirds of the melted chocolate onto a cool marble surface and stir the chocolate continually with a spatula or scraper to keep the chocolate moving until it starts to thicken (about 26°C/79°F). Crystallization is now taking place.

3   Pour the pre-crystallized chocolate from the marble surface into the rest of the melted chocolate (pic. a) and stir until it forms an even mixture. The temperature of the chocolate should now be adjusted to 32°C (90°F) for dark (semisweet) chocolate or 30°C (85°F) for milk or white chocolate.

a

The vaccination method

Pre-crystallization is easy if chocolate which has already been tempered is added to the melted chocolate – callets or small drops of chocolate are best for this. As the callets are already in the required crystallized form, when they melt into the chocolate they leave behind the crystals.

1 Melt the chocolate at a temperature of 45°C (110°F).

2 Add a small quantity of callets, and stir well until melted. (Pic. b.)

3 Check the temperature. If the temperature is above 32°C (90°F) for dark chocolate or 30°C (85°F) for milk or white chocolate add more drops and continue stirring until a smooth mixture at 32°C (90°F) or 30°C (85°F) is achieved. (Pic. c.)

Tempering in the microwave

This quick method is ideal when only a small amount of chocolate is required. Use callets or small chocolate pieces.

1 Pour callets or chocolate pieces into a microwave-safe bowl and place in the microwave.

2 Melt the chocolate at full power.

3 Take the chocolate out of the microwave every 15–20 seconds and stir well each time.

4 Continue until the chocolate has almost melted. Small drops should still be visible. (Pic. d.)

5 Remove from the microwave and stir until a slightly thickened, even liquid results. Adjust the temperature to 32°C (90°F) for dark (semisweet) chocolate or 30°C (85°F) for milk or white chocolate.

How to check pre-crystallization

Spread a tiny amount of chocolate on the tip of a palette knife or a piece of greaseproof (waxed) paper. If pre-crystallization has been achieved, the chocolate should harden evenly within 3 minutes at room temperature and display a good shine.

Thinning out Once chocolate has been tempered it must be used quickly. Because the chocolate is slowly crystallizing, after a time it will become 'over-crystallized' (i.e. too many crystals will form, causing it to thicken and become unusable). To keep the tempered chocolate workable, it must be thinned out. There are two ways to do this:

1 Slowly add melted, untempered chocolate to the tempered chocolate.

2 Use a heat source such as a hairdryer or paint stripper to melt any chocolate setting around the edge of the bowl, thus untempering it. This can then be stirred in to thin the chocolate.

With both methods it is critical that the working temperature is not exceeded. If the chocolate is accidentally over-warmed, the crystals will melt and the chocolate will require re-tempering.

Tip Before tempering chocolate, make sure you have all utensils, equipment etc. required to hand and any moulds or templates prepared.

COOLING

The ideal temperature for cooling chocolate is between 10–12°C (50–54°F) with good air circulation to remove heat during solidification. In warm weather items can be placed in the refrigerator to cool. It is important not to refrigerate the items for too long as they can become damp, causing sugar bloom, and can crack if they become too cold.

IMPORTANT ADVICE
Here are five tips for achieving perfect results:

1 Use 'good quality' chocolate, preferably couverture. Make sure it is fresh and uncontaminated by moisture, odours and oxidation.

2 If applicable, temper the chocolate correctly. This gives the shine and hardness.

3 If using moulds and acetates, make sure they are clean, dry and at room temperature.

4 Patience – do not rush chocolate. For that perfect shine it is better to cool items slowly and for longer.

5 Store chocolate products correctly – in an airtight package or container and in a dark, cool place.

TROUBLESHOOTING

PROBLEM	CAUSE/S	SOLUTION/S
Fat bloom (white colouration on the surface in the form of streaks and blotches)	• Cooling of the chocolate too slow • Poorly tempered chocolate • Over-crystallized chocolate	• See Cooling (page 9) • See Tempering (pages 8–9) • See Tempering (pages 8–9)
Thickening of chocolate whilst working	• Excessive crystallization of chocolate	• See Thinning out (page 9)
Difficulty in removal of chocolate from moulds	• Poorly tempered chocolate • Layer of chocolate too thin	• See Tempering (pages 8–9) • Use thicker layers or give an extra coating
Finished product not glossy	• Room or cooling too cold • Chocolate not tempered correctly • Moulds not cleaned sufficiently • Moulds too cold	• Remove from the refrigerator sooner, cool more slowly • See Tempering (pages 8–9) • Clean and polish moulds with a soft cloth • Warm moulds to room temperature before filling
Cracks in moulded products	• Cooling too fast and too cold	• See Cooling (page 9)
Fine white bloom on surface	• Sugar bloom	• See Storing chocolate (page 8)

Cakes and Sponges

Whilst the focus of this book is on making cakes that look impressive, it is vital that they taste wonderful too. Here are three recipes for delicious chocolate cakes and sponges (see page 12). Alternatively, you may already have your own favourite recipes. For each decorated cake I have specified which cake I have used, but any cake, and indeed any filling or covering, can be substituted. Basically a cake is a mix of four ingredients:

Flour Always use a soft flour. There are now some very good sponge (cake) flours available, which give a lighter sponge. Alternatively flour can be lightened by replacing a proportion of it with cornflour (cornstarch).

Fat Since the aeration in most recipes is partly achieved by the trapping of air via the beating, a fat with good creaming qualities is essential. Butter fails in this respect. A good cake margarine is therefore recommended.

Sugar Fine grain caster (superfine) sugar is most suitable, as it will readily dissolve in the batter.

Eggs Always use fresh eggs which are of a warm room temperature, 21°C (70°F). Cold eggs do not whisk or aerate very well.

Cocoa powder And, as this is a book about chocolate cakes, cocoa powder is the extra ingredient. Use the darkest, best cocoa powder you can find to give a quality chocolate flavour.

COMMON CAUSES OF BAKING MISHAPS

Cake sinks in the centre

1 Knocking in the oven prior to the cake setting. If, during cooking, the cake is disturbed when all the ingredients are in a fluid state, the centre may collapse.

2 Too much aeration. This is caused by adding too much baking powder or by overbeating the cake mix prior to adding the flour.

3 Undercooked. Make sure the cake is fully cooked by gently pressing the centre. If ready, it should spring back.

Peaked top

1 Flour used was too strong.

2 Oven too hot. Causes crust to form too quickly. The cake continues to rise producing a peaked top.

Small volume/close crumb and tough:
Insufficient aeration due to:

1 Insufficient beating of the batter or whisking of the eggs.

2 Mixture overbeaten, once the flour had been added.

3 Insufficient baking powder.

4 Eggs too cold.

LINING A CAKE TIN
Before baking any cake the tin must be prepared by lining it with greaseproof paper. This will facilitate the removal of the cake after baking.

Always oil the tin first by brushing vegetable oil sparingly over the base and sides. Then use one of the methods below depending on the shape of the tin.

Square tin Cut two strips of greaseproof (waxed) paper – width times width plus sides. Lay one strip to cover the base and two sides of the tin. Brush more oil on the base and lay the second strip the other way to cover the base again and the other two sides.

Round and shaped tins Lay the cake tin on greaseproof (waxed) paper and mark a line 1 cm (½ in) larger than the tin. Cut out this shape, then cut around the perimeter, 1 cm (½ in) deep every 2 cm (1¾ in). Lay the paper in the base of the tin and push the edges into the side. Then cut a second strip the height of the tin and lay it around the inside. For larger tins, several more of these strips may be required.

STORING CAKES
If well wrapped, cakes should retain their freshness for up to a week and if frozen, for up to three months.

Method 1
SUGAR BATTER METHOD
Makes 1 quantity

In this method aeration is achieved by the use of a raising agent (baking powder) in the flour and by beating the fat and sugar together.

- 450 g (1 lb/2 cups) margarine
- 450 g (1 lb/2¼ cups) caster (superfine) sugar
- Few drops vanilla essence
- 8 large eggs
- 365 g (13 oz/3¼ cups) self-raising flour
- 90 g (3½ oz/scant 1 cup) dark cocoa powder

1 Preheat the oven to 160°C (320°F/gas mark 3). Line the cake tin (see page 11).

2 Soften the margarine and beat with the sugar and vanilla essence until light and aerated.

3 Fold in the eggs, two at a time.

4 Combine the flour and cocoa powder. Sieve and fold into the mixture to form a smooth batter.

5 Pour into the tin and bake for approximately 1 hour.

6 To check whether the cake is cooked, gently press the centre of the cake with your finger, if it springs back, it is cooked.

7 Leave the cake in the tin to cool. When cool, remove from the tin, peel away the lining paper and wrap in cling film until required.

Method 2
QUICK-MIX
Makes 1 quantity

In this recipe aeration is also achieved by the use of baking powder and by beating the fat and sugar together.

- 175 g (6 oz/1½ cups) self-raising flour
- 50 g (2 oz/½ cup) cocoa powder
- 2 tsp baking powder
- 225 g (8 oz/1 cup) soft margarine
- 225 g (8 oz/generous 1 cup) caster (superfine) sugar
- 4 large eggs
- 2 drops vanilla essence

1 Preheat the oven to 160°C (320°F/gas mark 3). Line the cake tin (see page 11).

2 Sieve the flour, cocoa and baking powder into a large mixing bowl. Add the rest of the ingredients and beat until smooth.

3 The mixture should drop off a wooden spoon easily when tapped. If too thick add a little water and beat again.

4 Transfer the mixture into the lined cake tin and spread evenly with the back of a spoon. Bake for about 45 minutes.

5 Gently press the centre of the cake with your finger, if it springs back, it is cooked.

6 Leave the cake in the tin to cool. When cool, remove from the tin, peel away the lining paper and wrap in cling film until required.

Method 3
FLOUR BATTER METHOD
Makes 1 quantity

This cake is made in a food mixer. In this method, aeration is achieved solely by the air trapped in the eggs in the whisking process.

- 10 large eggs
- 450 g (1 lb/2 cups) margarine
- 360 g (13 oz/3¼ cups) plain (all-purpose) flour
- 90 g (3 oz/¾ cup) dark cocoa powder
- Few drops vanilla essence
- 500 g (1 lb 1½ oz/2½ cups) caster (superfine) sugar

1 Preheat the oven to 160°C (320°F/gas mark 3). Line the cake tin (see page 11).

2 Break the eggs into a warm mixer bowl and whisk on high speed until light and fluffy.

3 Whilst the eggs are whisking, melt the margarine in a saucepan. Remove from the heat. Combine the flour and cocoa powder and mix into the margarine. Beat until smooth. Add the vanilla and transfer to a large mixing bowl.

4 Add the sugar to the whisking eggs and continue beating until the sugar dissolves. Fold a third of this mixture into the fat/flour mixture. Then fold in another third and fold in the last third until a smooth batter is formed. Pour into the tin and bake for about 1 hour. Then follow steps 6 and 7 of the Quick Mix method.

Fillings All of these fillings are available to buy ready-made.

CHOCOLATE BUTTERCREAM
Makes 1 kg (2 lb)
The amount of chocolate is optional depending on how dark you like it.

- 225 g (8 oz/2 sticks) butter
- 225 g (8 oz/1 cup) margarine
- 350 g (12 oz) fondant (pouring fondant) (see page 14)
- 150–225 g (5–8 oz) melted dark bitter (bittersweet) chocolate

1 In a mixer, beat the butter and margarine together until smooth.

2 Add the fondant in small lumps whilst beating on a slow speed. Continue beating until light and aerated. Add the melted chocolate and beat in thoroughly.

GANACHE
Makes 1 kg (2 lb)
To use as a filling leave to set overnight, then beat and aerate. To use as a covering, leave in its liquid state.

- 400 ml (14 fl oz/1¾ cups) whipping cream
- 450 g (1 lb) dark (semisweet), milk or white chocolate, melted
- 120 g (4½ oz/1 stick) unsalted (sweet) butter, diced

1 Bring the cream to the boil in a pan and remove from the heat.

2 Add the chocolate to the cream, whisking until smooth. Beat in the butter until smooth.

TEA GANACHE
Makes 1 kg (2 lb)
Has a rich, dark chocolate taste.

- 600 g (20 oz) dark (semisweet) chocolate
- 400 ml (14 fl oz/1¾ cups) boiling water
- 2 tsp or 2 teabags Earl Grey tea
- Touch of orange water or grated orange zest

1 Melt the chocolate (see page 8).

2 Pour the boiling water onto the tea or teabags in a teapot/jug. Leave for 2 minutes and strain.

3 Slowly add the tea to the chocolate, whisking until smooth. Leave to set overnight.

PREPARING THE CAKE
Most chocolate cakes are filled with buttercream or ganache.

1 Prepare your filling, which should be of a soft, spreading consistency. If it has set too firm, warm it slightly and beat.

2 Trim the top of the cake level and turn it upside down. Secure onto a cake board with a little filling and place on a turntable. Place one hand on top of the cake and, using a carving knife, slice the cake horizontally, a third of the way down, while turning it (pic. a). Repeat to cut three equal slices.

a

3 Mark the front of the cake and board with a little filling. Remove the top two slices. Spread a thick, even layer of filling over the base with a palette knife. Place the next slice on, spread with filling and place the final slice on top. Make sure your markers align and that the sides are straight. Gently press a cake board on top to make sure it is level.

4 Spread the filling over the top and sides of the cake with a palette knife. Use a scraper and, holding the flat side vertically against the cake sides, turn the turntable until a smooth edge is formed (pic. b). Smooth the top with a palette knife, starting from the outside working in. Leave the cake to set for a couple of hours.

b

Coverings   All of these coverings are available to buy ready-made.

CHOCOLATE SUGARPASTE (ROLLED FONDANT)
Makes 800 g (28 oz)

Always keep sugarpaste wrapped in a plastic food bag to prevent it from drying out. It can be frozen if it is not going to be used for a while.

- 25 g (1 oz) egg white, made from powdered albumen
- 50 g (2 oz/¼ cup) liquid glucose
- 450 g (1 lb/3¼ cups) icing (confectioner's) sugar
- 225 g (8 oz/2 cups) cocoa powder
- 25 g (1 oz) white vegetable fat (shortening)

1 Mix the egg white and liquid glucose thoroughly.

2 Sieve the icing sugar and cocoa powder together. Add to the egg mixture and combine.

3 Turn the mixture onto a work surface and add the fat, kneading until smooth. Add more sugar if sticky or more fat if a bit dry.

COVERING A CAKE WITH SUGARPASTE (ROLLED FONDANT)

This method can also be used to cover a cake drum.

1 Sprinkle a clean work surface with icing sugar. Knead the sugarpaste until smooth and pliable. If the paste is cold, warm it slightly first. Form the paste into a ball, flatten and roll out. Keep the paste moving and continue sprinkling icing sugar underneath, as you roll out a circle large enough to cover the whole cake.

2 Roll the sugarpaste onto the rolling pin and, starting at the base of the cake, gently unroll it over the cake (pic. a).

a

3 Smooth the top with your hand or a cake smoother, before easing the paste down the sides. Trim off any excess with a plastic scraper (pic. b) and then smooth the sides with a smoother or a scraper. Gently polish the cake with the palm of your hand. If any air pockets appear, prick them with a pin and then smooth. Leave the cake overnight before decorating.

b

FONDANT (POURING FONDANT)
Makes 450 g (1 lb)

Fondant is basically crystallized sugar syrup, which can be flavoured. It is ideally suited to children's cakes as it is softer and sweeter than chocolate coatings and ganaches. Note that handmade fondant is never as white or as smooth as commercially manufactured fondant.

- 400 g (14 oz/2 cups) granulated sugar
- 150 ml (5 fl oz/⅔ cup) water
- 50 g (2 oz/¼ cup) liquid glucose

1 Over a gentle heat, stir the sugar and water until clear. Add the liquid glucose.

2 Raise the temperature and boil vigorously. Do not stir. Boil to a temperature of 115°C (240°F).

3 Pour onto an oiled marble slab and cool to around 40°C (100°F).

4 Agitate continually with a palette knife. As the syrup starts to crystallize, the mass will turn creamy and eventually turn thicker and whiter in colour.

5 When the mass is too thick to work with a palette knife, continue by hand, working it to a smooth paste. Store in an airtight container.

Equipment

Here is the basic equipment required. In the individual cake projects I have listed any extra equipment needed.

1. Marble slab Used for tempering chocolate and creating chocolate cigarellos and ruffles. A thick, smooth nylon chopping board can be used, but it will not stay cool for as long.

2. Metal comb scraper A scraper with zig-zag teeth used to create patterns in chocolate and icings.

3. Scrapers Used for a variety of purposes, from scraping out bowls to smoothing sugarpaste.

4. Palette knife Used for spreading chocolate, creams, icings etc.

5. Brushes Must be of food grade. Used for brushing oil and chocolate.

6. Scissors and knives A sharp pair of scissors is necessary to cut ribbon, greaseproof paper, acetate sheets etc. A variety of knives are used for cutting and trimming cakes and for cutting set chocolate.

Greaseproof (waxed) and (parchment) silicon paper Used for making piping bags, templates and for setting chocolate decorations on. It is best to use silicon paper when a stronger template is needed.

7. Acetate sheets Thin plastic sheets used for setting decorations where a high gloss finish is required.

8. Rolling pins A large rolling pin is needed to roll out sugarpaste for covering cakes and drums. A smaller nylon rolling pin is useful for rolling out small quantities of icing and modelling chocolate.

9. Chocolate thermometer A necessary tool for tempering. It must measure between 25–50°C (77–120°F).

10. Turntable Used to rotate cakes to facilitate cutting, layering and the application of decorations.

Mixing bowls If using a microwave oven use microwave-safe bowls.

11. Piping bags and nozzles Large nozzles and savoy bags are used to pipe choux pastry and decorations, whereas greaseproof paper piping bags are used to pipe chocolate.

Cake smoother Irons out lumps and bumps on a sugarpaste-covered cake.

Glue stick Used to fix ribbon in place on cake drums and boards. It must be non-toxic.

Double boiler Used to melt chocolate. A heatproof bowl placed over a saucepan can be used instead.

Ruler For measuring templates, ribbon, etc.

Cloths For cleaning cake boards and drums, polishing acetate strips, etc.

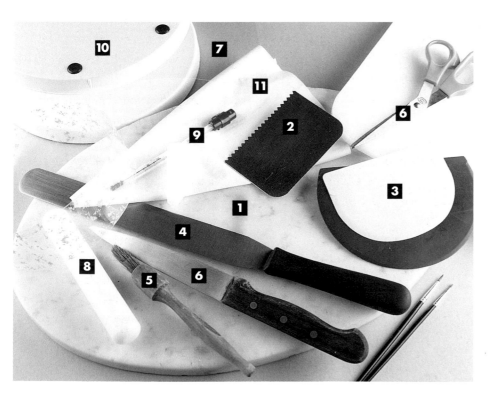

Praline Chequerboard Torte

Surprise and puzzle your friends with this cake. It looks much like any other until cut, when a delightful chequerboard patterned centre is revealed. The addition of praline adds a subtle hazelnut flavour.

YOU WILL NEED

- 1 quantity plain sponge mixture (Methods 1 or 3, see page 12, replace the cocoa powder with the same quantity of flour) baked in 20-cm (8-in) round cake tin
- 1 quantity chocolate sponge mixture (Methods 1 or 3, see page 12) baked in 20-cm (8-in) round cake tin
- 25-cm (10-in) round cake board
- 1 quantity chocolate praline buttercream (add 225 g (8 oz) praline paste, nutty chocolate spread or ground roasted hazelnuts to basic chocolate buttercream recipe, see page 13)
- 700 g (23 oz) chocolate sugarpaste (rolled fondant) (see page 14)
- 600 g (20 oz) baker's chocolate or chocolate-flavoured coating
- 250 g (8 oz) shiny chocolate callets
- 16 whole roasted hazelnuts
- 110 g (4 oz) dark (semisweet) chocolate, (for pipeouts, see page 18) or 16 shop-bought decorations

EXTRA EQUIPMENT

- Round cutters – 15 cm (6 in), 10 cm (4 in) and 5 cm (2 in)

Chocolate know-how

Chocolate couverture is recommended for the pipeouts as they will be stronger and easier to handle.

1 Trim the tops of the two cakes and slice in half horizontally. Now cut each slice into three circles using the cutters. Swap the middle circle in each slice so that the slices are now made up of chocolate and plain sponge circles (pic. a).

2 On the cake board prepare the cake and fill and coat with chocolate praline buttercream (see page 13), but alternate the slices (slice with outer chocolate circle, followed by slice with plain sponge outer circle etc.) to create the chequerboard effect.

3 Cover with a thin layer of chocolate sugarpaste (see page 14).

4 Melt the baker's chocolate (see page 8).

a

> **Chocolate is madness; chocolate is delight.**
>
> JUDITH OLNEY
> 20TH-CENTURY AMERICAN CHEF

b

c

5   Place the cake onto a turntable. Pour the melted chocolate over the top of the cake and spread smoothly and evenly over the cake and board using a palette knife (pic. b). If necessary, tap the turntable gently to level the coating. Neaten the edge of the board by drawing the palette knife downwards around the edge and wipe it clean with a dry cloth. Leave to set for at least an hour before decorating.

6   To decorate the base of the cake, brush a little melted chocolate around the base and attach the shiny callets to form a beading.

7   Place the remaining buttercream in a large piping bag and pipe rosettes around the edge using a large star nozzle (pic. c). Finally push a hazelnut and a pipeout/decoration (see below) into each rosette.

PIPEOUTS

d

1   Trace a row of motifs from the template on page 78 onto a piece of greaseproof paper.

2   Lay a sheet of acetate on top of the tracing.

3   Melt the dark chocolate (and temper if using couverture, see pages 8–9) and spoon a small amount into a greaseproof paper piping bag. Cut a small hole in the tip and pipe over the traced patterns (pic. d). Leave to set. Once set, remove the pipeouts from the acetate with a palette knife.

Chocolate pipeouts are a piped decorative pattern used commonly on tortes and gateaux.

Hedgehog

This cake is ideal for a children's party. It is quick and easy to make and most of it can be made a few days in advance.

YOU WILL NEED

- 32.5-cm (13-in) cake drum

- 400 g (14 oz) green sugarpaste (rolled fondant)

- 1 quantity chocolate sponge mixture (Methods 1 or 3, see page 12) baked in 25 x 20-cm (10 x 8-in) oval cake tin

- 30-cm (12-in) cake board

- 750 g (1½ lb) chocolate buttercream (see page 13)

- 750 g (1½ lb) chocolate sugarpaste (rolled fondant) (see page 14)

- 25 g (1 oz) white sugarpaste (rolled fondant)

- 12.5 g (½ oz) black sugarpaste (rolled fondant)

- 350 g (12 oz) milk chocolate, to make 50 cigarellos (see page 61) or 50 shop-bought cigarellos

- 1.5 m (4 ft) ribbon for cake drum

EXTRA EQUIPMENT

- Crimpers
- Small, round cutters

Chocolate know-how

Couverture is recommended for making the cigarellos, but other types of chocolate can be used.

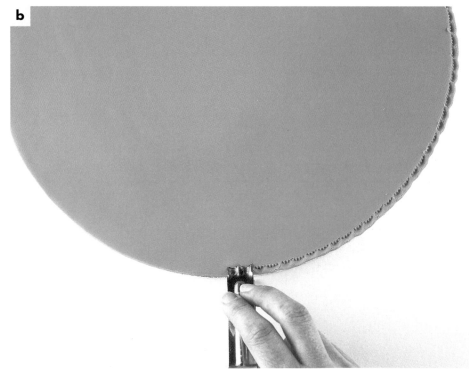

1 Cover the cake drum with the green sugarpaste (see page 14) and trim around the edge (pic. a). Decorate the edge using crimpers (pic. b) and put it to one side.

c

d

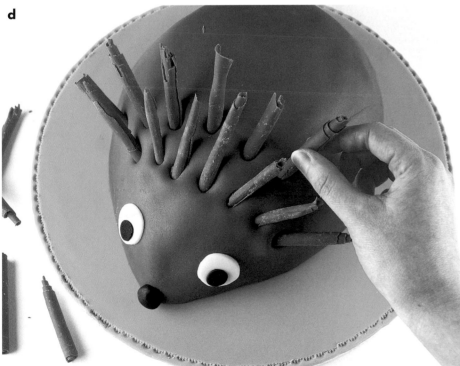

2 Place the cake on the cake board and, using a sharp knife, sculpt the cake into a hedgehog shape (pic. c). One end should narrow gradually to a soft point and the other end should be wider and more rounded. Cover the cake with buttercream (see page 13), then with a thin layer of chocolate sugarpaste (see page 14). Using a cake smoother, smooth the surface and trim the excess sugarpaste from around the sides. Leave it to firm overnight.

3 Carefully transfer the cake to the covered cake drum. Roll out the white and black sugarpaste. Cut circles for the eyes and make a ball for the nose. Attach with a brush and a little water.

4 Push the cigarellos firmly into the cake at an angle to make the spikes (pic. d). Start from the head and work backwards.

5 Measure and cut the ribbon to the correct length and attach it around the edge of the cake drum using a glue stick.

You know how I like to describe the way chocolate makes people feel? Watch a child devour a candy bar – that's contentment.

SANDRA RAMAGE
20TH-CENTURY AMERICAN CHOCOLATE LOVER

Chocolate Flower

This beautifully presented cake is one to be truly proud of. It is deceptively quick and simple to make and is suitable for any occasion.

YOU WILL NEED

- 1 quantity chocolate sponge mixture (Method 2, see page 12) baked in a 15-cm (6-in) round, deep cake tin
- 500 g (1 lb 1½ oz) chocolate buttercream (see page 13)
- 20-cm (8-in) round cake board
- 25-cm (10-in) round cake drum
- 350 g (12 oz) pale yellow sugarpaste (rolled fondant)
- 750 g (1½ lb) dark (semisweet) chocolate couverture
- Icing (confectioner's) sugar, for dusting
- 1 m (39½ in) ribbon for cake drum

EXTRA EQUIPMENT

- Round cutter

Chocolate know-how

Couverture is recommended, although other chocolate types can be used.

1 Prepare the cake on the cake board (see page 13). Fill and coat the cake with buttercream. Measure and note the height of the cake.

2 Cover the cake drum with the yellow sugarpaste (see page 14) and put to one side.

3 Temper the dark chocolate couverture (see pages 8–9) and make enough *langues de chat* to cover the outside of the cake (about 20; see page 24). Attach these to the outside of the cake using a little buttercream.

4 To make the curls to form the flower petals, spread a thin layer of tempered dark chocolate couverture onto a marble slab. When just set but not hardened, pull a round cutter towards you across the chocolate at an angle of 45 degrees to pare off petal shapes (pic. a).

a

" I do not remember at what age I brought my first chocolate cake into the world, although I will never forget the excitement and pride I felt on presenting it. "

PAMELA ASQUITH
20TH-CENTURY AMERICAN WRITER

b

5   Starting from the centre, arrange the petals on top of the cake working outwards to form a large flower (pic. b).

6   Lightly dust the top of the cake with icing sugar.

7   Transfer the cake to the cake drum. Measure and cut the ribbon to the correct length and attach it around the edge of the cake drum using a glue stick.

CHOCOLATE *LANGUES DE CHAT*

c

Called cat's tongues in English, these are very thin, tongue-shaped pieces of chocolate used to decorate cakes and gateaux, and as chocolate wafers in ice creams, sundaes and mousses.

1   Starting at the top of a sheet of greaseproof paper, draw two parallel lines. The lines should be the height of the cake plus 2.5 cm (1 in) apart. For example, if your cake is 15 cm (6 in) high, make the lines 17.5 cm (7 in) apart. Repeat until you fill the greaseproof sheet with parallel lines. Turn the greaseproof sheet over so that the marks are on the underside.

2   Dip the end of a palette knife into tempered, dark chocolate couverture and then, starting at the top line, drag it towards you to the next line (pic. c). The chocolate should become thinner as you drag down. It will take a few tries to work out how much chocolate is needed on the palette knife to achieve the desired length and thickness.

3   Leave to set hard before gently peeling the chocolate away from the paper.

Choc *Cherry Fondant*

Dark chocolate and cherries are a delicious combination especially when used with cherry brandy or kirsch. This cake is stunning, and is a fabulous dinner party dessert.

- 1 quantity chocolate sponge mixture (Method 2, see page 12) baked in a 20-cm (8-in) round cake tin

- 25-cm (10-in) cake board

- Approx. 400 g (14 oz) tinned black cherries or black cherry jam

- 500 g (1 lb 1½ oz) dark (semisweet) chocolate ganache (for filling, see page 13)

- 50 ml (2 fl oz/¼ cup) cherry brandy or kirsch (optional)

- 700 g (23 oz) chocolate sugarpaste (rolled fondant) (see page 14)

- 60 ml (2½ fl oz/generous ¼ cup) boiling water (for syrup solution)

- 110 g (4 oz/½ cup) granulated sugar (for syrup solution)

- 110 g (4 oz) dark (semisweet) chocolate

- 275 g (10 oz) fondant (pouring fondant) (see page 14)

- 110 g (4 oz) white chocolate

- 12–16 fresh cherries

EXTRA EQUIPMENT

- Jar

Chocolate know-how

Any type of chocolate can be used for this cake.

a

b

1 Prepare the cake on the cake board (see page 13). Fill with alternate layers of ganache and black cherries (or jam). Brush some cherry juice or cherry brandy on each layer to moisten and add flavour. Cover the cake with ganache.

2 Cover with a thin layer of chocolate sugarpaste (see page 14).

c

d

3 Place the cake on a turntable. To prepare the chocolate fondant icing (pic. a, shows the ingredients) make up a syrup solution by mixing the boiling water with the sugar, stirring until dissolved. Cool and store in a jar.

4 Melt the dark chocolate (see page 8).

5 Place the fondant in a double boiler with 2 tablespoons of the syrup solution and warm over a gentle heat whilst stirring until it is smooth. Do not let the temperature of the fondant go above 38°C (100°F). Overheating causes the minute sugar crystals to grow in size reducing their light reflecting properties and therefore their gloss. Stir in the melted dark chocolate and adjust the consistency with a little syrup, so that it is thin enough to find its own level after a few seconds.

6 Pour the fondant over the top of the cake and quickly smooth over the cake and the board using a palette knife (pic. b). Remove excess and leave to set for at least an hour before decorating.

7 Melt the white chocolate (see page 8). Half dip the cherries in the white chocolate and leave to set on greaseproof paper (pic. c).

8 Arrange the dipped cherries on top of the cake (pic. d).

Square
Box of Chocolates

Surprise your guests with the contents of this cake. Ideal for chocoholics, it's quick and easy to make. If you have more time or relish a challenge, try some of the pattern variations (see page 30) or make the Round Chocolate Box (see pages 40–43).

YOU WILL NEED

- 30-cm (12-in) square cake drum
- 500 g (1 lb 1½ oz) sugarpaste (rolled fondant) in a colour of your choice (for cake drum)
- 1 quantity chocolate sponge mixture (Methods 1 or 3, see page 12) baked in a 20-cm (8-in) square cake tin
- 30-cm (12-in) cake board
- 750 g (1½ lb) chocolate buttercream (see page 13)
- 350 g (12 oz) milk chocolate
- 350 g (12 oz) truffles
- 1.5 m (5 ft) ribbon for cake drum

Chocolate know-how

Any type of chocolate can be used for this cake.

1 Cover the cake drum with a very thin layer of coloured sugarpaste (see page 14).

2 Prepare the chocolate cake on the cake board (see page 13). Fill and coat with buttercream. Transfer it to the centre of the prepared drum. Take care not to get buttercream on the drum.

3 Make a template for the sides of the cake. Measure the width of the cake and then the height; add 2.5 cm (1 in) to the height. For example, for a 20-cm (8-in) wide by 7.5-cm (3-in) high cake, the template will be 20 cm (8 in) by 10 cm (4 in). Draw the template onto greaseproof paper. Cut out.

4 Melt the milk chocolate and spread a thin layer onto a large sheet of greaseproof paper with a palette knife (pic. a). The layer must be large enough to cut out four sides (see above). Leave until just set.

**Life is like a box of chocolates...
You never know what you're
gonna get.**

FORREST GUMP

5 Cut around the template with a large kitchen knife. Use a guillotine action to ensure neat edges (pic. b). Leave to harden.

6 Peel the sides from the greaseproof paper and stick them to the cake using a small amount of buttercream (pic. c).

7 Measure and cut the ribbon to the required length and attach around the cake drum using a glue stick.

8 Fill the top of the cake with a selection of truffles.

b

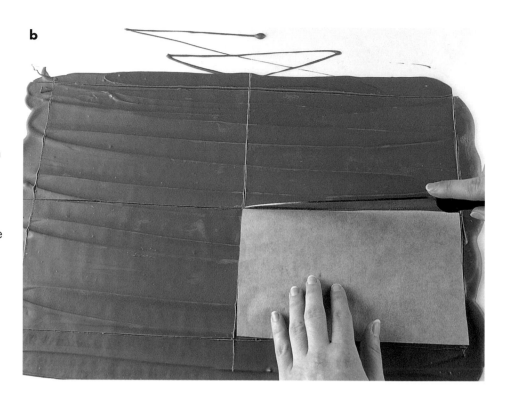

PATTERN VARIATIONS FOR THE CAKE SIDES

Circles After step 3 pipe random circles of white chocolate onto the greaseproof paper sheet. Leave until just set. Spread on the milk chocolate (see step 4) and follow steps 5–8.

Stripes After step 3 spread a thin layer of milk chocolate onto the greaseproof paper and run a comb scraper through it to create stripes. Leave until just set. Spread a thin layer of white chocolate over the stripes (see step 4) and leave to set. Follow steps 5–8.

Hearts After step 3, pipe heart shapes onto the greaseproof paper with white chocolate and leave until just set. Then spread on the milk chocolate (see step 4) and follow steps 5–8.

c

Ultimate
Chocolate Truffle Cake

Make this cake and challenge yourself or your guests to only eat one slice! Here, the very best bitter (bittersweet) chocolate is used to make this a truly irresistible cake.

YOU WILL NEED

- 1 quantity chocolate sponge mixture (Method 2, see page 12) baked in a 20-cm (8-in) round cake tin

- 2 quantities of tea ganache (see page 13), made using 70% dark (bittersweet) chocolate couverture

- 28-cm (11-in) round cake drum

- 750 g (1½ lb) dark (semisweet) chocolate couverture

- 250 g (9 oz) dark cocoa powder

- 1 m (39½ in) ribbon for cake drum

Chocolate know-how

To achieve the ultimate chocolate experience, couverture is strongly recommended for this cake. However, other chocolate types can be used.

a

1 Prepare the cake on the cake drum (see page 13). Fill and coat with ganache. Place in the refrigerator for a couple of hours to set.

2 Make the chocolate spikes using half of the chocolate (see above right).

3 Place the cake on a turntable. Resoften the remaining ganache until it is of a spreadable consistency. Use a palette knife to spread an extra thin layer of ganache over the side of the cake. Clean away any excess ganache from the cake drum. Use any left over ganache to make the truffles (see below right).

4 Attach the spikes by pushing them onto the side of the cake, overlapping them slightly (pic. a).

5 Melt and temper the remaining chocolate. Flood the cake drum (see page 61), and dip the truffles at the same time (see below right).

6 Arrange the truffles on top of the cake.

7 Measure and cut the ribbon to the required length and attach around the cake drum using a glue stick.

Strength is the capacity to break a chocolate bar into four pieces with your bare hands and then eat just one of the pieces.

JUDITH VIORST
WRITER

CHOCOLATE SPIKES

1 Temper the dark chocolate couverture (see pages 8–9).

2 Place an acetate sheet onto a flat surface and polish with a soft, dry cloth.

3 Using a palette knife, spread a thin layer of the couverture onto the acetate and leave in a cool place to set for at least an hour.

4 Peel the acetate away from the chocolate. Snap the chocolate into random, jagged pieces (pic. b) and trim the bases with a pair of scissors.

CHOCOLATE TRUFFLES

1 If necessary, warm the ganache to a soft, piping consistency. Transfer to a large piping bag fitted with a large, plain nozzle. Pipe amounts about the size of a large cherry onto a tray covered with greaseproof paper (pic. c). Chill in a refrigerator for at least two hours.

2 Using a fork, dip the ganache truffles in the dark chocolate (pic. d). Roll in cocoa powder and leave to set in a cool place.

3 Shake off the excess cocoa powder.

Chocolate Panel Cake

Using chocolate panels and fresh flowers for decoration, this is a quick and easy cake to make. It can be made with milk, white or dark (semisweet) chocolate; the example shown has been made with milk. The pattern variations for the sides of the Square Box of Chocolates (see page 30) could be used on this cake.

YOU WILL NEED

- 1½ quantities chocolate sponge mixture (Methods 1 or 3, see page 12) baked in 25-cm (10-in) and 17.5-cm (7-in) square cake tins

- 37.5-cm (14 ¾-in) square cake drum

- 1½ quantities milk chocolate ganache (for filling, see page 13)

- 17.5-cm (7-in) and 25-cm (10-in) square cake boards

- 1 kg (2 lb) milk chocolate

- Selection of fresh roses and leaves, for decoration

- 1.5 m (5 ft) ribbon for cake drum

Chocolate know-how

Any type of chocolate can be used for this cake.

1 Place the larger cake directly on the cake drum. Attach the 17.5-cm (7-in) cake to the 17.5-cm (7-in) cake board using ganache and then place on the larger cake board. Fill both cakes with ganache (see page 13). Make sure both cakes are approximately the same height. Leave to firm in a cool place for at least an hour.

2 Remove the smaller cake from the larger cake board and position on the larger cake, making sure that it is central and level.

3 Make the chocolate panels using 750 g (1½ lb) of the milk chocolate (see page 36).

4 Warm the remaining ganache slightly to soften it if necessary and then beat until light and soft. Using a palette knife, cover both tiers with a thick layer of ganache. Then use a scraper to smooth the sides and the palette knife to smooth the top.

For who can deny that when the taste buds are seeking excitement, drama and sweet satisfaction, it is neither the potato nor the cranberry to which we turn. It is chocolate.

LORNA J. SASS
AMERICAN HISTORIAN AND WRITER

5 Starting at a corner of the bottom tier, gently press the panels into place, slightly overlapping each one until all the sides are covered (pic. a).

6 Break any leftover panels into three pieces and fill in the tops of the tiers (pic. b).

7 Melt the remaining chocolate and use it to flood the cake drum (see page 61).

8 Ensure that the roses and leaves are clean. Fill the top of the first and second tier with roses and leaves.

9 Measure and cut the ribbon to the required length and attach around the cake drum using a glue stick.

CHOCOLATE PANELS

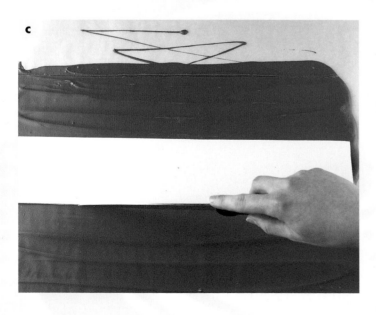

1 Measure the height of the bottom tier and make a card template the size of the width of your greaseproof paper by the height of the cake plus 1 cm (½ in).

2 Melt the chocolate (see page 8). Lay a sheet of greaseproof paper on a flat surface. Spread a thin, even layer of the chocolate over the paper and leave until just set.

3 Lay the template over the chocolate and, using a sharp knife, cut it into long strips (pic. c). Remove the template and cut the strips vertically into equal sized panels. Leave to harden for at least one hour.

4 Remove the chocolate panels from the paper.

Bitter
Fruity Ganache Cake

This is a colourful cake that combines the bitterness of dark (semisweet) chocolate with the sweet tang of fruits. It provides a perfect and refreshing finish to any meal.

- 1 quantity chocolate sponge mixture (Method 2, see page 12) baked in a 20-cm (8-in) round cake tin

- 28-cm (11-in) round cake drum

- ½ quantity dark (semisweet) chocolate ganache (for filling and coating, see page 13)

- 600 g (20 oz) chocolate sugarpaste (rolled fondant) (see page 14)

- ½ quantity dark (semisweet) chocolate ganache (for covering, see page 13)

- 500 g (1 lb 1½ oz) dark (semisweet) chocolate couverture

- Selection of summer fruits

- 1 m (39½ in) ribbon for cake drum

- Round bucket (or saucepan) approx. 25 cm (10 in) in diameter

Chocolate know-how

Couverture is recommended for making the delicate decorations for this cake and is therefore referred to in the recipe. However, any chocolate type can be used.

a

b

1 Prepare the cake (see page 13) on the cake drum. Fill and coat with the ganache. Cover with a thin layer of chocolate sugarpaste and place on a turntable.

2 Make a fresh ganache and whilst still warm, pour over the cake and use a palette knife to spread an even smooth coat over the cake and drum. Leave to set for at least an hour. Neaten the edge of the drum using a knife and wipe clean with a cloth.

3 Temper the dark chocolate couverture (see pages 8–9). Make the chocolate background and waves (see page 39). Make a selection of chocolate leaves in various sizes (see page 61).

4 Push the chocolate background into the back of the cake.

5 Fill the top of the cake with summer fruits, cascading them down to the cake drum (pic. a). Add the chocolate waves and leaves (pic. b).

6 Measure and cut the ribbon to the required length and attach around the cake drum using a glue stick.

Good living is an act of intelligence by which we choose things which have an agreeable taste rather than those which do not.

BRILLAT-SAVARIN – FRENCH GOURMET

CHOCOLATE BACKGROUND

1. Lay an A4 acetate sheet on a flat surface and polish with a soft, dry cloth. Spoon some of the chocolate couverture onto the acetate and, using a palette knife, spread out thinly into a rectangle shape 15 cm (6 in) high by 20 cm (8 in) wide. Then make a pattern in the chocolate by zig-zagging the palette knife, starting at the top and working down (pic. c). Try and overlap the chocolate at the bottom of the acetate to give the background a flat base.

2. Place the chocolate-covered acetate sheet into the bucket, bottom first. Leave to set in a cool place for at least an hour.

3. When set hard, remove the chocolate-covered acetate sheet from the bucket and gently peel away the acetate. Store in a cool place until required.

CHOCOLATE WAVES

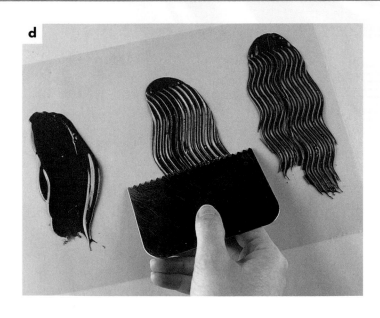

1. Place an A4 sheet of acetate on a flat surface and polish it with a soft, dry cloth.

2. Dip the end of a palette knife into the chocolate couverture, then touch it onto the acetate sheet and draw the knife towards you until the chocolate tapers away.

3. Pull a comb scraper towards you at an angle of 45 degrees through the chocolate, starting 5 mm (⅕ in) from the far end, moving it from side to side as you go to produce a wavy effect (pic. d). Repeat until the acetate sheet is covered.

4. Leave the waves to set hard for at least one hour in a cool place, before gently peeling them away from the acetate sheet.

Round
Chocolate Box

This is slightly more challenging than the Square Box of Chocolates (see pages 28–30). Fill it with an irresistible selection of your favourite chocolates. The pattern variations suggested for the Square Box of Chocolates can also be used for this cake.

YOU WILL NEED

- 28-cm (11-in) round cake drum
- 350 g (12 oz) pink sugarpaste (rolled fondant) (for cake drum)
- ½ quantity chocolate sponge mixture (Methods 1 or 3, see page 12) baked in a 15-cm (6-in) round, deep cake tin
- 2 x 25-cm (10-in) round cake boards (spares, to be used for preparation)
- 350 g (12 oz) chocolate buttercream (see page 13)
- 650 g (21 oz) dark (semisweet) chocolate couverture
- 17.5 cm (7-in) round cake board
- Chocolate bow (see page 43)
- 225 g (8 oz) chocolates/truffles
- 1 m (39½ in) ribbon for bow around cake
- 1 m (39½ in) ribbon for cake drum

EXTRA EQUIPMENT

- 23-cm (9 in) round piece bubblewrap

Chocolate know-how

Couverture is recommended to make the delicate decorations for this cake.

1 Cover the cake drum with a very thin layer of coloured sugarpaste (see page 14).

2 Prepare the cake (see page 13) on one of the larger spare cake boards. Fill and coat with buttercream.

3 Make a template from silicon paper by measuring the circumference of the cake plus 5 mm (⅛ in), by the height plus 2 cm (¾ in). (E.g. for a 15-cm/6-in wide by 10-cm/4-in cake, the template would be 47.5 cm/ 18¾ in by 12 cm/5 in.)

4 Temper the dark chocolate couverture (see pages 8–9). Spread a thin layer (2–3 mm) over the template with a palette knife. Leave until just starting to set (pic. a, page 42).

5 Neaten the edges with a knife and curve around the side of the cake and join (pic. b, page 42).

6 To make the lid of the chocolate box, spread a 3-mm (⅛-in) layer of chocolate onto the cake card (pic. c, page 42) and leave it to set hard.

Chocolate! Now that is a word that conjures up describable ecstasies.   Truffles, bonbons...cakes, cookies and more. Breathes there a man, woman or child who has not lusted after it, devoured it, and moments later dreamed of it still?

ELAINE GONZALEZ
20TH-CENTURY AMERICAN ARTIST.

a

b

c

d

7 To make the base, lay the bubblewrap (bubble-side up) onto the other spare cake board and spread a generous layer of the chocolate on top to form a circle 2 cm (¾ in) smaller than the bubblewrap (pic. d). Tap the underside of the cake board to release any air bubbles. Leave the chocolate to set hard.

8 Remove the lid from the cake card. Assemble the chocolate bow on the lid with a little melted chocolate (see page 43).

9 Turn the base upside down and gently peel away the bubblewrap. Attach the base onto the covered cake drum with a little buttercream.

10 Carefully transfer the cake onto the centre of the base by sliding it gently off the cake board.

11 Peel away the silicon paper template. Fill the top of the box with chocolates/truffles and place the lid on top.

12 Tie a bow around the chocolate box.

13 Measure and cut the ribbon to the required length and attach around the cake drum using a glue stick.

BOWS

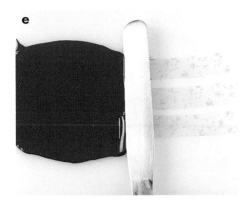

Bows are an impressive and versatile decoration, yet they are straightforward to make. Your bow can have around 7–11 loops, and tails can be added as you wish. This step-by-step example uses acetate which is ready-embossed with an edible pattern.

1 Use the loop and tail templates on page 78 to cut the acetate into the appropriate shapes.

2 Place on a marble slab or flat surface and polish with a soft, dry cloth.

3 Spread a thin, even coat (approx. 3 mm/⅛ in) of tempered chocolate across the strips using a palette knife (pic. e).

4 Lift the strips and run your fingers down the sides to give a neat edge.

5 To make the loops, press the ends together (pic. f) and place under a weight on greaseproof paper and leave to set for at least an hour.

6 Allow the tails to set on a flat surface.

7 To make the base, spread a 4-cm (2-in) circle of chocolate on grease-proof paper and leave to harden.

8 When the loops have hardened, peel away the acetate to reveal the embossed pattern (pic. g). Trim the ends. Starting with three loops, dip the ends in chocolate and arrange them, evenly spaced, on the base. Leave them to set. Gradually form the bow by adding 3–5 more loops, a couple at a time and leaving them to set, until the bow is complete.

PATTERN VARIATIONS

Striped Spread dark chocolate over the acetate strips and draw a comb scraper through the chocolate to form stripes. When just set, spread white chocolate over the whole area with a palette knife. Continue with steps 4–8.

Patterned Pipe random circles of dark chocolate over the acetate strips and, when just set, spread white chocolate over the whole area. Continue with steps 4–8.

Dotted Pipe dots of dark chocolate on the acetate strips and, when just set, spread white chocolate over them. Continue with steps 4–8.

Valentine's Love Heart

Treat the one you love with this delightful cake on Valentine's Day, you could even pipe on a personal and romantic message. To complement the red roses I have used a dark (semisweet) chocolate coating.

YOU WILL NEED

- 1 quantity chocolate sponge mixture (Method 2, see page 12) baked in a 20-cm (8-in) heart-shaped cake tin
- 28-cm (11-in) heart-shaped cake drum
- 500 g (1 lb 1½ oz) tea ganache (see page 13)
- 700 g (23 oz) chocolate sugarpaste (rolled fondant) (see page 14)
- 600 g (20 oz) dark (semisweet) chocolate couverture
- 175 g (6 oz/1½ sticks) butter
- 100 g (4 oz) white chocolate
- 50 g (2 oz) dark (semisweet) chocolate
- 3 red sugarpaste (rolled fondant) roses (see page 58)
- Chocolate leaves (see page 61)
- 1 m (39½ in) ribbon for cake drum

EXTRA EQUIPMENT

- Heart cutter

Chocolate know-how

Couverture is used as a covering for this cake. Any chocolate type can be used for making and attaching the heart cut-outs and leaves.

1 Prepare the cake on the heart-shaped cake drum. Fill and coat with ganache (see page 13). Cover with a thin layer of chocolate sugarpaste and smooth using a cake smoother.

2 Place the cake on a turntable. Prepare the dark chocolate couverture covering (see page 46). Pour over the top of the cake and spread evenly over the cake and drum using a palette knife (pic. a). Tap the turntable gently to level the coating. Neaten the edge of the drum by drawing the palette knife downwards around the edge (pic. b) and wipe clean with a dry cloth. Leave to set for at least an hour before decorating.

3 Half-fill a greaseproof paper piping bag with melted chocolate and cut a hole in the tip. Using this chocolate, attach the heart cutouts (see page 46) at an angle around the base of the cake. Arrange the roses and leaves on top of the cake and attach with a little chocolate (pic. c).

4 Measure and cut the ribbon to length and attach it around the cake drum using a glue stick.

Giving chocolate to others is an intimate form of communication, a sharing of deep, dark secrets.

MILTON ZELMAN,
PUBLISHER OF *CHOCOLATE NEWS*

CHOCOLATE CUTOUTS

Chocolate cutouts are a quick and simple decoration which are made using cutters of various shapes and sizes. Here the method for cutout hearts is described.

1 Melt a quantity of dark and white chocolate.

2 Spoon a small amount of dark chocolate into a greaseproof paper piping bag and cut a small hole in the tip. Pipe thin random squiggles on an acetate sheet or greaseproof paper and leave until just set.

3 Spread a thin layer of white chocolate across the whole area (pic. d).

4 When just setting, cut out shapes with a heart-shaped cutter (pic. e). Leave to harden in a cool place for at least one hour. When cutting out the shapes, if the cutter sticks this is because the chocolate is still too soft. If the chocolate cracks, it is set too hard.

5 Carefully remove the hearts from the paper or acetate.

COUVERTURE FOR COVERING CAKES

Couverture is too hard for coating cakes. It cracks when set and splinters when cut. However, if softened, it makes an ideal cake covering. To soften the couverture, a soft fat such as butter or vegetable oil is added.

1 Clarify the butter by melting and allowing it to settle for a few minutes. The fat separates and rises to the top leaving the watery liquid at the bottom. When separated, carefully pour the fat into a jug leaving the watery liquid behind in the pan to be discarded.

2 Temper 600 g (20 oz) dark chocolate couverture (see pages 8–9). Add the clarified butter and stir in.

Vertical Layer Torte

This torte is assembled in a unique way which, when served, reveals a clever and eye-catching vertical pattern. The cake shown right has been filled with white chocolate so that you can see the pattern clearly.

YOU WILL NEED

- Vegetable oil, for greasing baking tray
- 1 quantity Genoese sponge mix (see page 49)
- Caster (superfine) sugar, for sprinkling
- 30-cm (12-in) round cake board
- 750 g (1½ lb) chocolate buttercream (see page 13)
- 50 ml (2 fl oz/¼ cup) dark rum (optional)
- Cocoa powder, for sprinkling
- 250 g (8 oz) dark (semisweet) chocolate

EXTRA EQUIPMENT

- 40 x 25-cm (15 x 10-in) baking tray
- Strip of card for template, the depth of the cake hoop
- 25-cm (10-in) cake hoop

Chocolate know-how
Any chocolate type can be used for this cake.

1 Preheat the oven to 220°C (430°F/gas mark 7). Brush a little oil on the baking tray and line with greaseproof paper. Make the sponge mix and pour into the tray and spread evenly. Bake for approximately 5 minutes until the middle of the sponge springs back when pressed. While the sponge is baking, lay a sheet of greaseproof paper on your work surface and liberally sprinkle it with caster sugar. When the sponge is baked, remove from the oven and turn it out upside down onto the sugared paper. Leave the baking tray on top allowing the steam to moisten the sponge. When cooled, remove the tray and peel away the greaseproof paper.

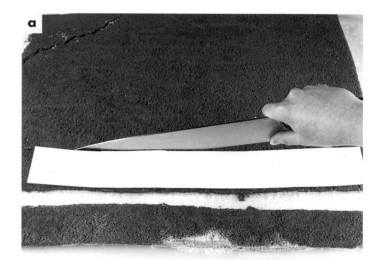

2 Using the card template as a guide, cut the sponge into even strips (pic. a). Spread buttercream over the strips.

3 Place the cake hoop onto the cake board and insert the first strip of sponge (buttercream side facing in) around the inside of the hoop. Continue inserting the strips (pic. b) spiralling inwards until you reach the centre. If liked, gently pour the rum evenly over the top. Cover the cake top with a layer of buttercream and smooth the surface flat with a palette knife (pic. c). Dust the top with cocoa powder. Clean any surplus powder from the cake board with a damp cloth. Refrigerate until the buttercream hardens.

c

d

4 Run a knife around the inside of the hoop to loosen the sponge. Remove the hoop and cover the sides with a thin layer of buttercream.

5 Melt the dark chocolate (see pages 8–9).

6 Lay a 1-m (39½-in) long acetate strip onto a flat surface and polish with a soft, dry cloth. Spread a thin layer of the dark chocolate over the acetate strip. Once the chocolate starts to set, wrap the chocolate strip around the cake.

7 Half-fill a greaseproof paper piping bag with dark chocolate and cut a small hole in the tip. Pipe a pattern of random circles on top of the cake (pic. d).

8 Leave the cake in a cool place for one hour, before peeling away the acetate strip from the side of the cake.

GENOESE SPONGE MIX

Aeration in this sponge is achieved solely by the air trapped in the eggs in the whisking process.

- 8 large eggs
- 250 g (8 oz/generous 1 cup) caster (superfine) sugar
- 250 g (8 oz/2 cups) plain (all-purpose) flour, sifted

1 Using an electric whisk, whisk the eggs on a fast speed until light and fluffy.

2 Add the sugar and continue beating until the sugar dissolves.

3 Using a large spoon, very carefully fold in the flour.

'...we should rejoice that a chocolate dessert can bring so much innocent pleasure, even when a little wickedness is insinuated.

MARCEL DESAULNIERS
CREATOR OF THE 'DEATH BY CHOCOLATE' DESSERT.

Yule Log

This cake is a firm favourite with many of my customers at Christmas. It makes a fine alternative to a traditional fruit cake, mince pies or Christmas pudding.

YOU WILL NEED

- Vegetable oil, for greasing
- 1 quantity Genoese sponge mix (see page 49)
- Caster (superfine) sugar, for sprinkling
- 50 ml (2 fl oz/¼ cup) dark rum (optional)
- 30-cm (12-in) round cake board
- 750 g (1½ lb) chocolate buttercream (see page 13)
- 150 g (6 oz) neutral marzipan
- 500 g (1 lb) dark (semisweet) chocolate
- Icing (confectioner's) sugar, for dusting
- Decorations – holly, robins etc.

EXTRA EQUIPMENT

- 40 x 25-cm (15 x 10-in) baking tray
- 8-cm (3-in) round cutter

Chocolate know-how

Couverture is recommended for the cigarellos, but other chocolate types can be used. You could use shop-bought cigarellos.

1 Preheat the oven to 220°C (430°F/gas mark 7). Brush a little oil on the baking tray and line with greaseproof paper. Make the sponge mix, pour into the baking tray and spread level. Bake for approximately 5 minutes until the middle of the sponge springs back when pressed. While the sponge is baking, lay a sheet of greaseproof paper on a table and liberally sprinkle it with caster sugar. When the sponge is baked, turn it upside down onto the sugared paper. Leave the baking tray on top allowing the steam to moisten the sponge. When cooled, remove the tray and peel away the greaseproof paper. Gently pour on the dark rum if required.

2 Spread an even layer of buttercream over the sponge (pic. a) and, holding the greasproof paper, roll it up to form a Swiss (jelly) roll (pic. b, page 52).

a

In the beginning, the Lord created chocolate, and he saw that it was good. Then he separated the light from the dark, and it was better.

ANONYMOUS

DRAPES

1 Place the dowels on a clean, flat surface 2.5 cm (1 in) apart. Roll out a strip of sugarpaste 30 x 10 cm (12 x 4 in). Lay it over the three dowels.

2 Run the end of a paintbrush down between the dowels to form a ridged effect (pic. c).

3 Remove the dowels and pinch one end of the sugarpaste together (pic. d). Trim if needed. Attach this end to the top of the cake with a little water and position it so that it drapes down to the bottom of the middle tier.

c

d

4 Repeat with a smaller drape (roughly 20 x 10 cm/8 x 4 in) and position it spiralling down from the top of the bottom tier to the drum.

ROSES

1 To make a realistic rose, prepare three slightly varying shades of chocolate modelling paste.

2 Warm the paste slightly in the microwave and knead it until smooth.

3 Take a ball of paste and model it into a bud shape on a base.

e

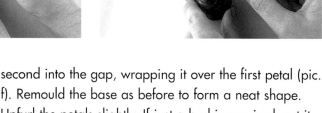
f

4 To make the first petals, roll three smooth balls of the darkest paste 1 cm (½ in) in diameter. Place them between two sheets of polythene and, using your thumb and finger, gently press, working from the centre outwards to form a round petal. The middle should be thicker and the edges very thin.

5 Wrap the first petal around the bud to completely cover the tip (pic. e). Remould the base of the bud to retain the original shape.

6 The next stage requires two petals. Wrap the first around the bud leaving one side curled back. Tuck the

second into the gap, wrapping it over the first petal (pic. f). Remould the base as before to form a neat shape. Unfurl the petals slightly. If just a bud is required, cut it from the base with a pair of scissors.

7 Repeat step 4, but this time using three petals and a lighter shade of paste. Wrap each petal around the bud. Reform the base and unfurl the petals. Again, the rose can be cut just below the base.

8 For larger roses, add a further four petals in the same fashion using the lightest paste. In most displays a selection of various sizes is required. Buds are very useful for filling any gaps.

White Wedding Dream

This is a popular contemporary wedding cake design. The white chocolate decorated with roses is particularly effective but fresh flowers or summer fruits work just as well.

YOU WILL NEED

- 3 kg (6½ lb) white chocolate couverture (for cigarellos, see page 61)
- 3 quantities chocolate sponge mixture (Methods 1 or 3, see page 12) baked in 30-cm (12-in), 22.5-cm (9-in) and 15-cm (6-in) round cake tins
- 40-cm (16-in) round cake drum
- 30-cm (12-in) and 20-cm (8-in) round cake drums (for preparation)
- 22.5-cm (9-in) and 15-cm (6-in) round cake boards
- 2 kg (4 lb 4 oz) dark (semisweet) chocolate ganache (see page 13)
- 1½ kg (3 lb 3 oz) white chocolate ganache (see page 13)

- 100 ml (4 fl oz/½ cup) brandy or your favourite liqueur
- 250 g (9 oz) white chocolate (for flooding cake drum, see page 61)
- Selection of pink modelling chocolate roses (see pages 57 and 58; make white modelling chocolate and colour it pink using food paste colour)
- 150 g (5 oz) milk chocolate (for leaves, see page 61)
- 1.5 m (4.5 ft) ribbon for cake drum

Chocolate know-how

Couverture is recommended for making the cigarellos (you can, of course, use shop-bought ones). Any chocolate type can be used for the other aspects.

1   Make the chocolate cigarellos (see opposite).

2   Fill and coat the cakes (see page 13) with dark chocolate ganache. Prepare the largest cake on the 40-cm (16-in) cake drum. Attach the smaller cakes to the same size cake boards with dark chocolate ganache and then place them onto the spare cake drums for preparation. Leave for a couple of hours in a cool place until the ganache sets.

3   Stack the cakes on top of one another making sure that they are central and level.

4   Warm the white chocolate ganache slightly and beat until light and soft. Liqueur can be added to give extra flavour. Using a palette knife and scraper, cover the entire cake with a thick layer of white ganache (pic. a).

5   Starting with the bottom tier, neatly press the cigarellos into the side of the cake making sure they are vertical and are tightly packed together. Repeat for the middle and top tiers.

6   Break up any spare cigarellos and use them to fill the tops of the cake tiers.

7   To flood the cake drum melt the white chocolate (see page 8) and follow the instructions opposite.

8   Arrange the roses and leaves around the cake and attach with a little melted chocolate.

9   Measure and cut the ribbon to the required length and attach it around the cake drum using a glue stick.

Forget love - I'd rather fall in chocolate!!!

ANONYMOUS

CHOCOLATE CIGARELLOS

Chocolate cigarellos are a very popular form of decoration which can be used for a variety of purposes. They can be made in advance and then stored in an airtight container in a dark, cool place.

1 Temper the chocolate couverture (see pages 8–9).

2 Spread a thin layer of the chocolate onto a marble slab or nylon chopping board. (The slab or board may become too warm and will need to be cooled periodically in the refrigerator.)

3 When just setting but not hard, push a metal scraper through the chocolate at an angle of 45 degrees to form long cigarellos (pic. c). For a neat finish, roll the cigarellos gently on a flat surface using your hand.

CHOCOLATE LEAVES

1 The most effective way to make chocolate leaves is to use real leaves as a mould. Check that the leaves are safe to use for this purpose and are not poisonous. Find thick, smooth leaves and wash and dry them thoroughly. Brush melted chocolate on the underside of the leaves and leave to set hard (pic. d).

2 Very carefully peel the leaves away from the chocolate.

FLOODING THE CAKE DRUM

1 Use a palette knife to spread a layer of chocolate all around the cake drum, smoothing as you go.

2 Clean the edge of the cake drum with the palette knife and then with a dry cloth.

Fairy Cake *Tower*

This fun cake can be decorated and presented in so many different ways and is becoming popular for all occasions. Because it comprises individually prepared cakes, serving is especially quick and easy!

1 Preheat the oven to 160°C (320°F/gas mark 3).

2 Prepare the cake mixture. Using a large piping bag fitted with a large, plain nozzle, half-fill the muffin cases with the cake mixture (see pic. a).

3 Bake for 12 minutes until the mixture has risen to fill the cases and is firm to touch. Allow the cakes to cool.

4 Using a small knife, cut out the tops of the cakes and keep to one side. Fill the holes by piping in a little buttercream (pic. b, page 64). Replace the tops.

a

> Chocolate candies are the best. Sweet and dark, they melt on our tongues and linger in our mouths with a delicious warm creaminess that is part taste, part memory.

MARY GOODBODY
20TH-CENTURY AMERICAN WRITER

b

c

5 Boil the apricot jam with a little water and whisk until smooth. Brush the hot jam over the tops of the cakes.

6 Knead the chocolate sugarpaste until it is smooth and roll it out to a thickness of 3 mm (⅛ in). Use the cutter to cut out circles and position them on top of the cakes (pic. c). Smooth the tops with your hand.

7 Make your chosen decorations and attach them with a little melted chocolate or buttercream.

8 Arrange the cakes on the cake stand.

CHOCOLATE RUNOUTS

d

e

A chocolate runout is a common decorative effect. It is a useful technique for creating a variety of shapes. Any type of chocolate can be used.

1 Using the template on page 78, trace the butterfly onto greaseproof paper. Trace as many times as you need. Turn the tracing over.

2 Melt some dark chocolate and spoon a small amount into a greaseproof paper piping bag. Cut a small hole in the tip and pipe over the tracing of the butterfly and leave to set.

3 Melt some milk chocolate and half-fill a piping bag. Cut a slightly larger hole in the tip. Pipe the chocolate to flood the areas inside. (Pic. d shows the three stages.) Leave the runout to set for at least an hour.

4 Remove the wings from the paper. Fold a piece of card to make an upright 'M' shape and line the centre (the 'V') with greaseproof paper. Place the wings on the greaseproof paper and pipe a line of chocolate down the centre of each butterfly to join and form the body (pic. e).

Chocolate Croquembouche

A croquembouche is the traditional French wedding cake made with layers of choux buns dipped in caramelised sugar built up around a central cone. Here I have adapted the original recipe to create a chocolate version. The base and cone can be made in advance, the filling the day before and the choux buns made on the day.

- 45-cm (18-in) square piece of card for cone
- 35-cm (14-in) round cake drum
- 1 kg (2 lb) dark (semisweet) chocolate
- 2 kg (4 lb 4 oz) white chocolate ganache (see page 13)
- 100 ml (4 fl oz/½ cup) liqueur (optional)
- 1.25 m (4 ft) ribbon for cake drum
- Decorations can include any or all of the following: almonds, pipeouts (see page 18), runouts (see page 64), cutouts (see page 46), bows (see page 43)

For 60 Choux pastry buns:

- 250 g (9 oz/2¼ sticks) butter cut into cubes
- 600 ml (1 pt) water
- Pinch salt
- 15 g (½ oz/2 Tbsp) caster (superfine) sugar
- 500 g (1 lb 1½ oz/4½ cups) strong white (unbleached white bread) flour, sieved
- 8 large eggs
- Vegetable oil, for greasing

EXTRA EQUIPMENT

- Adhesive tape
- Large baking sheet

Chocolate know-how

Any chocolate type can be used for this cake.

BASE AND CONE

1 To make the cone, roll the card into a cone shape and secure with adhesive tape. The cone should be approximately 50 cm (20 in) tall.

2 Trim the base so that it stands up straight. Then, cover with greaseproof paper and secure, again with adhesive tape.

3 Melt half of the chocolate. Attach the cone to the cake drum with the melted chocolate and then brush a thin coat of melted chocolate over the whole cone and the drum (pic. a).

MAKING THE FILLING

4 The day before, make a white chocolate ganache for the choux bun filling and allow it to set.

5 On the day, warm the ganache slightly to soften. Transfer it to a mixer and beat until light and aerated. Liqueur can be added for extra flavour.

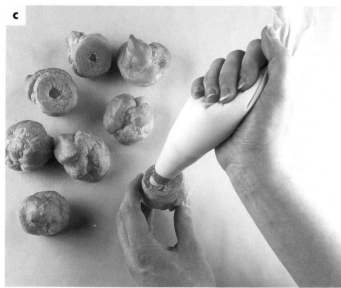

CHOUX BUNS

6 Heat the butter, water, salt and sugar in a saucepan until it comes to the boil.

7 Stir in the flour with a wooden spoon. Continue to stir the mixture until it is smooth and leaves the sides of the pan. Remove the mixture from the heat and allow it to cool slightly.

8 Beat in the eggs one at a time. The paste should be soft but it will need to retain its shape when piped.

9 Preheat the oven to 200°C (400°F/gas mark 6).

10 Pipe the mixture through a large piping bag fitted with a large piping nozzle onto a lightly greased baking sheet (pic. b). (You will need to bake the buns in batches.)

11 Bake for approximately 30 minutes until the buns are well risen and golden brown. As a general rule, when you think the buns are cooked, leave them in for a couple of extra minutes. If the buns are removed from the oven too soon they will collapse and soften.

12 Make a small hole in the base of each bun with a small piping nozzle.

13 Put the white chocolate ganache into a large piping bag fitted with a small nozzle. Pipe the filling into the choux buns (pic. c).

14 Melt the remaining dark chocolate (see page 8). Dip the base of the buns in the chocolate and attach them to the cone one layer at a time (pic. d), starting at the bottom working up to the top. Allow each layer to set before continuing.

15 Measure and cut the ribbon to the required length and attach around the cake drum using a glue stick.

16 Attach your chosen decorations with a little melted chocolate.

Forever Frills

This design will appeal to those wanting a chocolate wedding cake with a traditional feel. The bows, flowers and frills on the cake are bound to thrill the bride, groom and guests.

YOU WILL NEED

- 2 quantities chocolate sponge mixture (Methods 1 or 3, see page 12) baked in 30-cm (12-in) and 20-cm (8-in) round cake tins

- 35-cm (14-in) and 27.5-cm (11-in) round cake boards (for preparation)

- 1½ kg (3 lb 3oz) chocolate buttercream or ganache (see page 13)

- 2.75 kg (6 lb) chocolate sugarpaste (rolled fondant) (see page 14)

- 40-cm (16-in) and 27.5-cm (11-in) round cake drums

- 350 g (12 oz) dark (semisweet) chocolate couverture for 12 leaves, 2 bows (see pages 61 and 43), piping

- 500 g (1 lb 1½ oz) white and milk chocolate modelling paste (see page 57) for frills and selection of chocolate roses in various shades of brown (see page 58)

- 2 m (6½ ft) ribbon for cake drums

EXTRA EQUIPMENT

- 4 x 7-cm (3½-in) round, ivory cake pillars
- 4 x 20 cm (8 in) plastic dowels
- Garrett frill cutter
- Cocktail stick

Chocolate know-how

Couverture is recommended to make the bows and leaves. Any chocolate type can be used for the piping and for attaching items.

1 Prepare the larger cake on the 35-cm (14-in) board and the smaller cake on the 27.5-cm (11-in) board. Fill and coat the cakes with buttercream or ganache. Cover both cakes with chocolate sugarpaste (see page 14). Leave overnight to harden.

2 Cover the cake drums with the remaining sugarpaste (see page 14) and leave them overnight to dry.

3 Carefully slide or lift the cakes onto the centre of the covered cake drums.

4 To position the cake pillars, cut a 12-cm (5-in) square of greaseproof paper and place it in the centre of the cake. Make a mark at each corner of the

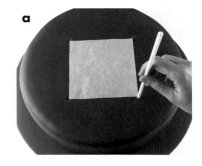

paper using a dowel (pic. a). Remove the template and position the pillars on these marks. Push a dowel through a pillar and the cake to the drum. Mark the dowel, level with the top of the pillar, using a knife (pic. b, page 70). Remove the dowel and score around the mark with a knife. The dowel should now snap cleanly. Cut the other dowels to the same length. Position all of the pillars on the cake, push the dowels in and secure the pillars with a little chocolate.

5   Pipe beading around the base of the cakes using dark chocolate (see pic. b, page 57).

6   Make the frills (see below). Attach the frills to each cake with melted chocolate, starting at the top and working downwards until you reach the base (pic. c). Arrange the milk chocolate frills 0.5 cm (¼ in) above the white loops.

7   Using dark chocolate, pipe beading on the upper edge of the frills.

8   Arrange the bows, roses and leaves, securing them with melted chocolate.

9   Measure and cut the ribbon to the correct lengths and attach around the cake drums using a glue stick.

10 Place the top tier onto the pillars.

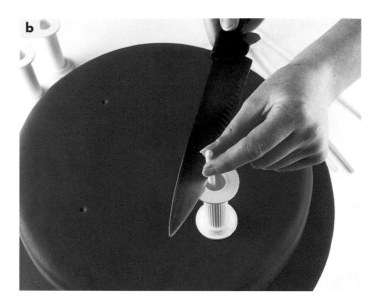

"

......truly wonderful masterpieces can be created with great skill and all will be acclaimed with great enthusiasm, simply because they are made of chocolate.

JENNIE REEKIE
20TH-CENTURY ENGLISH HOME ECONOMIST "

FRILLS

1   Knead the white chocolate modelling paste and roll out thinly. Use the garrett frill cutter to cut out the frills.

2   Using a cocktail stick, roll firmly around the edges to create the frill effect (pic. d). Cut the frill open with a knife and open into a loop.

3   Repeat stages 1 and 2 using milk chocolate modelling paste.

Easter
Basket

This cake is perfect for Easter but the idea can also easily be adapted for Mother's day or a birthday. It is simple to make but requires the handle and the daffodils to be made a week in advance.

Chocolate know-how

Any chocolate type can be used for this cake.

THE DAFFODILS

The flowers are best made up to a week in advance. Once hardened they are easier to handle.

1 Colour half of the white chocolate modelling paste yellow and the other half green.

2 To make the leaves, roll out the green paste and, using a sharp knife, cut out approximately seven leaf shapes (see template page 78). Mark the veins with a sharp knife. Bend the top of some of the leaves over and place them to one side.

3 To make the flowers, roll out the yellow paste. Using the daffodil petal cutter, cut out six sets of petals and neaten the edges with your fingers.

4 To make the trumpets, cut out six shapes using a trumpet cutter or use the template on page 78. For each trumpet, form a tube by overlapping one end over the other. Seal the ends together by gently rolling the inner seam with a cocktail stick. Roll a cocktail stick on one of the edges of the tube to frill it out (pic. a). Attach to the petals using edible glue.

THE HANDLE

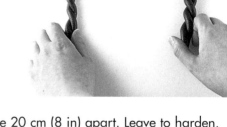

The handle must be made in advance and left for at least a week in a cool, dry place to harden and strengthen.

5 Make a rope 45 cm (18 in) long (see opposite) using dark modelling chocolate. Shape the rope to form the handle (pic. b) and adjust the ends so that they are 20 cm (8 in) apart. Leave to harden.

ASSEMBLING THE CAKE

6 Cover the cake drum with the green sugarpaste (see page 14).

7 Prepare the cake on the cake board (see page 13). Fill and coat the cake with buttercream. Measure and note the height of the cake.

c

(5 in). Loosely roll up the paste then unroll it around the side of the cake. Trim the ends if necessary and join using a pastry brush dampened with a little water. Leave overnight to allow the sugarpaste to harden.

10 Transfer the cake onto the covered cake drum.

11 Using dark chocolate modelling paste, make two ropes at least 63 cm (25 in) in length (see below). Wrap the first rope around the base of the cake, trim to length and join. Wrap the second rope around the top of the basket, trim to length and join. Attach these with a little melted chocolate if necessary.

8 Knead the chocolate sugarpaste and the marzipan together until smooth. The marzipan gives the sugarpaste more strength and rigidity. Roll the paste out into a rectangle at least 60 cm (24 in) by 15 cm (6 in) wide. Then roll over the paste, lengthways, firmly with the basketweave rolling pin to mark the basket pattern (pic. c).

12 Dip the last 4 cm (1.5 in) of each end of the handle in melted chocolate and attach to the basket. Support the handle until set.

9 Using a sharp knife, trim the rectangle to size using this formula: circumference of the cake by the height of the cake plus 2.5 cm (1 in). For example, for a round cake 20 cm (8 in) wide by 10 cm (4 in), the sugarpaste will need to be 63 cm (25 in) by 12.5 cm

13 Fill the basket with chocolate eggs.

14 Using a little melted chocolate, attach the daffodil leaves, followed by the flowers to the side of the basket.

15 Measure and cut the ribbon to the required length and attach it around the cake drum using a glue stick.

ROPE

d

1 Use chocolate modelling paste and warm slightly in the microwave and knead until smooth. Divide it into two equal quantities.

2 Gently roll out half of the paste into a long sausage shape. Continue rolling until it is long and thin. Repeat with the other half.

3 Press the two strips together side by side. Then, twist the ends in opposite directions to form a rope (pic. d). If necessary, trim the ends to length with scissors.

Tower of Flowers

I designed this style of cake for my own wedding and want to share the idea with you. Designing your own wedding cake makes the day even more special and it gives you the chance to really impress.

YOU WILL NEED

- 3 quantities chocolate sponge mixture (Method 2, see page 12) baked in 3 x 17.5-cm (7-in) round cake tins
- 35-cm (14-in) round cake drum
- Cointreau (optional)
- 1 kg (2 lb) tea ganache (see page 13)
- 2 x 17.5-cm (7-in) round cake cards
- 1 kg (2 lb) white chocolate ganache (see page 13)
- 1.25 kg (2¾ lb) white chocolate couverture
- 350 g (12 oz) white sugarpaste (rolled fondant) coloured pale yellow, using food paste colour, to match the white chocolate
- 25 red roses and 15 green leaves made from sugarpaste (rolled fondant) or white modelling chocolate coloured with food paste colours (see page 58)
- 2 chocolate bows with tails (see page 43)
- Chocolate heart cutouts (see page 46)
- 1.25 m (4 ft) ribbon for the cake drum

EXTRA EQUIPMENT

- Long plastic dowel

Chocolate know-how
The effects used in this cake can only be achieved using chocolate couverture.

1. Trim the tops of all three cakes so that they are level. Slice each cake into three equal layers. Take the first cake and place the first slice on the cake drum. Sprinkle it with Cointreau (if desired) and spread an even layer of tea ganache over the top. Repeat for the second slice, then spread a very thin layer of ganache on the top of the third slice.

2. Insert the dowel through the centre of the cake, to the drum. Cut a hole in the centre of one of the cake cards and lower it over the dowel and onto the cake (pic. a).

3. Take the second cake and layer the next three slices as before but push each cake slice over the dowel. After the sixth slice, cut a hole in the centre of the other cake card and lower it over the dowel.

a

Flowers speak the language of love for some, but for others, it's chocolate that fans the flames.

REBECCA J. PATE
20TH CENTURY AMERICAN CHEF

4 Repeat with the third cake layering the final three slices as before. You should now have a very tall column comprising three layered cakes separated with two cake cards.

5 Using a palette knife, cover the entire cake with white ganache and smooth with a scraper (pic. b).

6 Temper 350 g (12 oz) of white chocolate couverture (see pages 8–9). Using a pastry brush, cover the bottom 8 cm (4 in) of the cake with a thin layer of the chocolate (pic. c). This gives the cake stability. Flood the drum with the rest of the chocolate (see page 61).

7 Make the chocolate strips (see above right) and position them on the cake as soon as they are made. Wrap the strips around the cake by overlapping them, starting at the top and working downwards (pic. d).

8 Make the ruffles (see below right) and attach around the top of the cake to form a large ruffle (pic e).

9 Knead the pale yellow sugarpaste, shape into a dome and push it over the dowel, onto the top of the cake.

10 Melt a small quantity of white chocolate and use it to attach:

- the roses to cover the dome. Bunch them closely together to ensure there are no gaps.
- the chocolate bows and tails to the sides of the cake.
- the chocolate heart cutouts.

11 Finally, measure and cut the ribbon to the required length and attach around the cake drum using a glue stick.

CHOCOLATE STRIPS

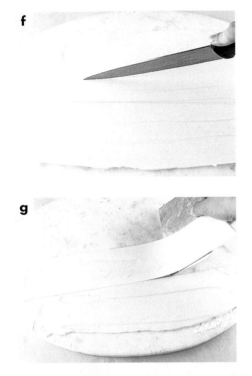

f

g

Chocolate strips are made using untempered chocolate couverture worked on a frozen marble slab. Speed is of the essence when using this method, as the slab remains frozen for only a short time and needs to be re-frozen at regular intervals. As a consequence, the strips need to be made in small batches.

1 Place the marble slab in the freezer and leave overnight.

2 Melt the remaining white chocolate couverture (see page 8). Pour a ladle of the chocolate onto the frozen slab and quickly spread it out with a palette knife. It will start to set almost immediately.

3 Using a sharp knife quickly cut the chocolate into long strips (pic. f).

4 Slide a metal scraper under the chocolate to peel a strip away from the slab (pic. g). Repeat until you have covered the cake. Position the strips on the cake whilst they are still pliable.

CHOCOLATE RUFFLES

h

These are made using a similar method to the strips.

1 Repeat steps 1 and 2 above.

2 Cut strips approximately 7 x 30 cm (3 x 12 in).

3 Remove the strips from the slab one at a time using the scraper, concertina each one and then squash one end to form a fan shape (pic h). Attach them to the cake whilst they are still pliable.

Templates All shown at actual size.

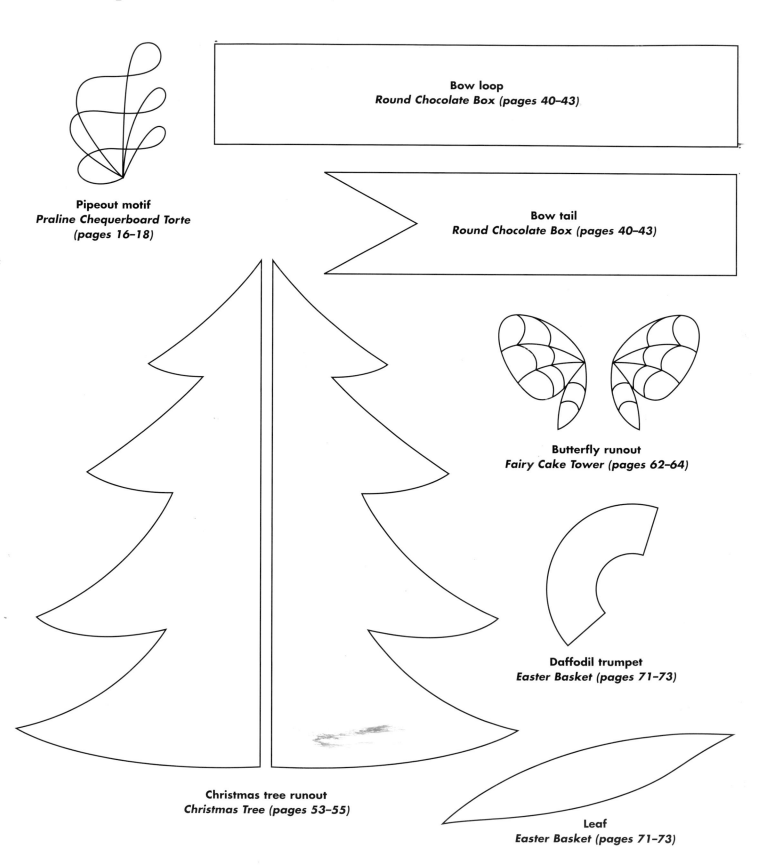

Pipeout motif
Praline Chequerboard Torte
(pages 16–18)

Bow loop
Round Chocolate Box (pages 40–43)

Bow tail
Round Chocolate Box (pages 40–43)

Butterfly runout
Fairy Cake Tower (pages 62–64)

Daffodil trumpet
Easter Basket (pages 71–73)

Christmas tree runout
Christmas Tree (pages 53–55)

Leaf
Easter Basket (pages 71–73)

Suppliers

UK

Barry Callebaut (UK) Ltd
www.barry-callebaut.com
Manufacturer of high-quality cocoa, chocolate and confectionery products.

Culpitt Ltd
Tel: 01670 814545
www.culpitt.com
Freephone enquiry line:
0845 601 0574
Distributor of cake decorating supplies; telephone for your nearest retail outlet.

Hannah's Sugarcraft
Tel: 01509 416638
www.quorndon.com/hannahs/
Wide range of cake decorating accessories and equipment.

Jane Asher Party Cakes
Tel: 020 7584 6177
www.jane-asher.co.uk
Range of equipment for sale, cake tins and stands for hire.

London Sugarart Centre
Tel: 020 8767 8558
Everything for the cake decorator - cake tins, cake decorating equipment and accessories.

SOUTH AFRICA

Cape Town

The Baking Tin
52 Belvedere Road
Claremont 7700
Cape Town
Tel: (021) 671 6434

South Bakels
55 Section Street
Paarden Eiland 7420
Cape Town
Tel: (021) 511 1381

Johannesburg

Chocolate Den
Shop 35, Glendower Shopping
Centre
99 Linksfield Road
Glendower
Edenvale 1609
Johannesburg
Tel: (011) 453 8160

South Bakels
235 Main Road
Martindale 2092
Johannesburg
Tel: (011) 673 2100

Party's, Crafts and Cake Decor
Shop 4, East Rand Mall
Riettontein Road
Boksburg 1459
Johannesburg
Tel: (011) 823 1988

Durban

The Baking Tin
Shop 108, Glenwood Village
Cnr Hunt & Moore Road
Glenwood 4001
Durban
Tel: (031) 202 2224

Port Elizabeth

The Baking Tin
Rochel Road
Perridgevale 6001
Port Elizabeth
Tel: (041) 363 0271

South Bakels
Section 9 Pogson Park
Podson Street
Sydenham 6001
Port Elizabeth
Tel: (041) 453 5397

Bloemfontein

South Bakels
19 Henry van Rooijen Street
Bloemfontein 9301
Tel: (051) 432 8446

NEW ZEALAND

Baker Boys South City
Shop 26 South City Centre
Christchurch
Tel: (03) 379 9100
Bakers, cake decoration supplies, cake shops.

Cake Craft and Decorating Suppliers
122 Grange Road
Otumoetai, Tauranga 3001
Tel: (07) 576-0075
Fax: (07) 576-0075
www.cakecraft.co.nz

Chocolate Boutique
3/27 Mokoia Rd Birkenhead
Auckland
Tel: (09) 419 2450
Cake decoration supplies, confectioners, gift baskets.

Dee Sees Creations Ltd
PO Box 21 111, Flagstaff,
Hamilton
Tel: (07) 854 3039
Cake decoration supplies.

Golding Handcrafts
Harbour City Centre, Lambton
Quay, Wellington
Tel: (04) 472 4496
Cake decoration supplies.

Havelock Bakery
57 Havelock Ave, Palmerston
North
Tel: (06) 354 3569
Bakers, cake decoration supplies.

Sugarcrafts NZ Ltd
99 Queens Rd, Panmure,
Auckland
Tel: (09) 527 6060
Cake decoration supplies, cake shops

Sweetpea Creations Ltd
P.O. Box 65 011 Mairangi Bay
Auckland
Tel: (09) 479 4132
Cake decoration supplies.

Sweet Treat
Queens Arc, Lower Hutt
Tel: (04) 569 6842
Cake decoration supplies, confectioners.

Voong's Bakery
Shop 7, 5 McMillan Ct,
Newlands, Wellington
Tel: (04) 478 3223
Bakers, cake decoration supplies, cake shops.

Chocolate Suppliers

Chocolate Boutique
Shop 1 323 Parnell Rd Parnell
Auckland
Tel: (09) 377 8550
www.chocolateboutique.co.nz
Chocolate, corporate gift baskets, hot chocolate, desserts, coffees, handmade chocolate, confectionery, gourmet foods.

de Spa Chocolatier
www.despa.co.nz
Exquisite Belgian chocolates made in New Zealand, corporate gifts, sugar-free selection, assortment of handmade truffles.

AUSTRALIA

NSW

Bakery Sugarcraft
Unit 7/1 Cowpasture Place
Wetherill Park NSW 2164
Tel: (02) 9756-6164
Fax: (02) 9756-6165

QLD

Cake & Icing Centre
651 Samford Road
Mitchelton, QLD 4053
Tel: (07) 3355 3443

SA

Classic Cake Decorating Centre
359 Tapleys Hill Rd
Seaton SA 5023
Tel: (08) 8353 4021

WA

Major Cake Decoration Supplies
Shop 2, 900 Albany Hwy
East Victoria Park WA 6101
Tel: (08) 9362 5202

VIC

West's Cake Decorations Pty. Ltd.
15 Florence St
Burwood VIC 3125
Tel: (03) 9808 3999

TAS

Gum Nut Cake & Craft Supplies
3 Haber St
Midway Point TAS 7171
Tel: (03) 6265 1463

Index